Human Nature

The Elephant in the Room as Humanity Faces Catastrophic Climate Change

Miles Sherts

an Nature

Copyright © 2020 Miles Sherts

ISBN 978-0-9854359-3-6 (print)

Published by Sky Meadow Press

To contact the author or purchase this book:
www.PracticalPresence.org
www.MilesSherts.com

Printed in the United States of America

Disclaimer

This book is for educational purposes. The views expressed are those of the author. The reader is responsible for his or her own actions. Neither the author nor the publisher assumes any responsibility or liability whatsoever on the behalf of the reader of these materials. The information, ideas, and techniques in this book are not advice or treatment, but rather knowledge intended to assist the reader to make informed decisions.

Contents

Introduction

Let's begin with these observations.

- By relentlessly extracting and consuming the natural resources of our planet and dumping the resulting waste back into our living environment, we are undermining our survival as a species.
- We have disrupted Earth's carefully balanced ecosystems to the point that the atmosphere of our planet is destabilizing, and we are disabling Earth's ability to sustain us.
- Although most of us are now aware of this, and our science has proven it, we are still not able to stop ourselves from destroying the conditions for life on Earth.

And let's end with a conclusion.

- The problem is not a lack of knowledge, resources, information, or technology. The problem is that our fundamental human nature seems to be self-destructive, and most of us don't believe we can do anything about that.

Stuck in a Rut

I have been on a track of personal growth and change, which I describe as a spiritual path, for over forty years. Early in life, I saw how toxic my mind was and dedicated myself to changing that and helping others do the same. I assumed that everyone would see this as clearly as I did, and that we would all want to change and grow to become more conscious, aware, and alive. And it is just now dawning on me that most of the people I encounter don't believe that personal growth or change is possible.

Most of us like the idea of becoming more disciplined, mature, and wise. We want to be better people and have tried reforming our basic human nature. But a lot of us gave up when our dedicated efforts didn't change anything. There seemed to be some ingrained force of habit that blocked our intelligence, and despite our best intentions, we ended up repeating the same self-destructive behaviors.

Human nature is the "elephant in the room" that few people are talking about in the discussion of climate change. We appear to be stymied in our efforts to resolve this crisis by our own ingrained habits. We can have the best intelligence, the most advanced technology, and the most creative ideas, but without fundamentally changing the way we think and act, we remain helplessly stuck on our tragic path of self-annihilation.

This should come as no surprise. Our basic human nature has always been self-destructive. Knowing that something is killing us, like excessive smoking, drinking, or eating, is not enough to make us stop. Our habits foil us in the end, and we seem powerless to do anything about it. The only thing new here is that we are seeing it on a global scale that makes it painfully evident that there is something fundamentally wrong with us.

I know you wince at that suggestion, as I do. We want to defend human goodness and intelligence and look away from the horrifying precipice we are poised to throw ourselves off. But it's too late for denial or avoidance. The problem is too big and looming now to pretend it doesn't exist. Our habit of turning away from ugly truths about ourselves is what brought us to this brink. So, let's try to learn something from this impossible situation, shall we?

Intelligence?

How can conscious beings like us possibly do such a thing as to destroy the environment that we depend on for life? What kind of intelligence would knowingly undermine the survival of its own species, to compete for a moment of wealth, power, fame, or semblance of security? How did we get here?

We like to think of ourselves as intelligent, and compared with other life forms here on Earth we do seem to have more capacity for rational thought and precise observation. Yet we often lack the ability to change our behavior, even when we know it will result in our own demise.

When we see someone doing something self-destructive, like getting hooked on drugs, alcohol, or tobacco, or eating to the point of obesity, we might scratch our heads in disbelief, shrug our shoulders, and ask, "How could they be that stupid?" It's easy to see that person as someone who can't take care of themselves, and their behavior is usually not of any great consequence to us.

However, in the case of global climate change caused by our ever-increasing emissions of CO_2 into our atmosphere, the problem is on a whole different scale. This behavior is already affecting all of us in some way and has the potential to destroy the conditions for life on Earth. And a majority of us are still unwilling or unable to change, despite increasingly dire warnings from our scientists and organizations charged with looking out for humanity's best interests.

It seems that a basic definition of intelligence would be that we would change our behavior once we knew that it was causing our own destruction. Our collective inability to respond to the increased warnings of the effects of global climate change suggests that we lack some basic intelligence, and our capacity for rational thought is not enough. If we are about to destroy the environment we depend on for our life, we must have some learning and growing to do to become truly intelligent.

A Way Out

This book is for those of us who are paying attention, see the looming disaster, feel how hopeless it appears, and still have the courage to seek for answers. There must be something we don't see yet—some secret or mystery hidden beneath this absurd turn of events— some message behind this madness.

This writing is not meant to discourage or overwhelm anyone with despair. It is simply that we must face the reality of our situation—that we are knowingly causing the climate on our precious planet to destabilize and undermining its capacity to support us and all of life. It is only by looking right at this alarming truth that we have any chance of learning from our mistakes.

I believe that we not only *can* change our human nature, but it is the reason we are here. Our main responsibility in this life is to recognize that our basic nature is fatally flawed and to grow beyond it. That is what Earth is for, it is why we all came here, and the global climate crisis that threatens to swallow all of us is demonstrating that in no uncertain terms.

However, we must be smart about how and where we can actually effect change. It should be obvious by now that we can't think our way out of this, or even will our way out of it. Governments and legislatures can put up boundaries against our most destructive habits, if and when they are able, but this will only slow the destruction. We still all have to do the work to change our nature, or we will simply find ourselves back here again in time.

To find a real resolution to this crisis requires that we actually grow and mature. This book will explore the root cause of our self-destructive nature and reveal a solution that is as simple as it is radical. It does not involve taking up a new belief system or religion, repeating affirmations, or relying on supernatural forces. It does require a level of self-awareness and insight into the workings of our own consciousness that will be a stretch for many. But this is the journey we came here to take, whether we recognize it or not.

The Message of Climate Change

In the past, human crises were largely contained within a community, nation, continent, or region. A famine, war, corrupt government, or natural disaster does not affect us directly unless we live in the vicinity. And if we are not affected, then it is someone else's issue.

As our awareness grew about environmental pollution in the 1960s, however, the notion of isolated problems began to change. We realized that coal-fired power plants in the Midwest of the US were creating acid rain along the East Coast, and that throwing waste into rivers contaminated them far downstream. And in the past several decades, it has become increasingly clear that our emissions of CO_2 are changing the entire atmosphere surrounding Earth and causing the climate of the whole planet to warm and become less stable.

The underlying message of this crisis is that we are all connected. We are all in the same boat, tethered to planet Earth and dependent on it for our survival. What happens to Earth's atmosphere affects us all.

Before this crisis, Earth seemed so vast and diverse that we focused mainly on our differences and saw ourselves in competition with one another for survival. Now our perspective is rapidly changing as we recognize that Earth is a living organism that is finite, fragile, and vulnerable. We all belong to it as it belongs to us, and without it we cannot survive.

From a spiritual point of view, this is a positive shift. We are beginning to see that our fate is tied to the fate of every other person and living being on Earth, and we are not separate in our own worlds as we thought. The global climate crisis is illustrating in no uncertain terms that we are all part of one Earth, and what one of us does here impacts everyone else.

Our individual egos want nothing to do with this new perspective and will deny or ignore it as long as possible, because it diminishes our autonomy. Yet, our hearts welcome this new perspective, because it dispels the illusion of separation and resolves the pain of isolation. This is the silver lining here. This crisis needed to happen to demonstrate that we all belong to one another, and we are not separate and alone, as we thought.

Learning from Our Mistakes

We are seriously discussing artificial intelligence that would supersede the human mind, biogenetically engineering people, and colonizing Mars in the event that Earth can no longer support life. The reality of human-created global climate change has finally dawned on us, and the mind-numbing realization that this entire planet could fail is freaking us out.

Meanwhile, our greatest Western liberal democracies are being split apart and deconstructed by competing ideologies; increasing fundamentalism is threatening to throw us back into an age of warring tribes, and inconceivable random acts of violence are undermining any sense of security or sanity in our daily lives. This perfect storm of impossible situations has made many of us hopeless, depressed, and suicidal, while others are putting their faith in technology to save the day.

It is time for us to come to our senses. I don't mean to limit our creativity, but let's be smart about where to put our focus. Promoting desperate ideas, like colonizing Mars, offers solace in pure fantasy.

There is only one Earth that we know of. Look at the other planets in our own small solar system, and it is apparent how rare a planet like Earth is that can support life. Of course, there likely are other inhabitable planets somewhere in the universe, but we lack the means to get to them. It would be a stretch for us today to fly a crewed spacecraft to our own small moon again. There really is nowhere we can go to escape from this problem.

But more to the point, if *we* are causing the disintegration of Earth's ecosystems and possibly rendering it uninhabitable, that sobering fact should be getting all of our attention. How could intelligent beings like us *do* such a thing? *How did we get here?*

If we don't use our intelligence to answer this question, we will inevitably repeat the same self-destructive behaviors wherever we go. True intelligence begins with learning from our mistakes and correcting our actions accordingly, as any artificial intelligence expert will tell us.

Before we can learn from our mistakes, however, we must first admit them. Our habitual response to crisis is to blame someone else. Once we figure out whose fault it is, we do whatever we can to get *them* to change. As most of us know from experience, trying to get other people to change their behavior can feel like hitting our head against a brick wall. It uses an enormous amount of effort, often requires force or coercion, and frequently fails completely.

This strategy is the cause of endless power struggles between us, which often lead to violence and war. No one likes to be pressured to change against their will, and most of the time each side in a conflict sees the other as the one responsible for causing the problem, thereby justifying any means to use against them. Even in those rare occasions where we do succeed in changing someone else's behavior, the problem inevitably surfaces again, because we have only addressed the symptoms, not the actual cause.

The Problem

So, what is the cause, you might ask? It is obviously our human nature. When we exhaust ourselves by blaming others and playing the victim, at some point we reach a level of honesty and recognize that the problem is our own irrational behavior, rather than an outside force pitted against us. We might not ever admit this, especially to our adversaries, but most of us know in our hearts that we often contradict what is in our own best interest.

As much as we like to see ourselves as rational and intelligent, we are mostly emotional and compulsive. Knowing that something is harmful to us, doesn't stop us from doing it. We all seem to be under the control of a maniacal ego that just does what it wants, despite our best intentions. And there seems to be nothing we can do to change this.

Just be honest with yourself for a moment and recognize something you do that you know is not good for you. Maybe you eat too much sugar, drink too much alcohol, don't get enough sleep, smoke tobacco, can't put down your phone, or don't exercise enough. We all do these things, and then try to hide them from ourselves, thinking we can trick ourselves into believing we only do what is good for us.

Reading that last paragraph probably made you uncomfortable. Bringing to mind habits you have that don't serve you is difficult because it makes you feel shame or guilt, triggering self-judgment and condemnation. This is why you work so hard to forget about your transgressions against your own health and well-being. Your peace of mind seems to depend on pretending that you are perfectly rational and would never knowingly do something that might hurt you in the long run.

My intention in putting a spotlight on our irrational behavior is not to cause more pain, but to begin the process of healing. When we hide from ourselves, we are split internally and our vital energy is fragmented in a way that debilitates us. The first and most difficult step in regaining integrity is self-awareness and honesty. When we can no longer fool ourselves, we are coming back into alignment with our wholeness, and beginning to regain our full power and strength.

When we hold tight to our belief that the problem is someone or something else, we never get to see the self-destructive behaviors that are programmed into us, and we can't do anything to change them. We will forever feel helpless and without power, and our lives will feel aimless and empty, with only the righteous fight we are waging against the obvious perpetrators of evil to keep us going.

So, it is imperative now that we be honest enough with ourselves, and eventually with one another, to admit that our inherent human nature is the real problem here. Despite knowing for decades that we are destroying the ecosystems we depend on for our survival, we have not been able to stop ourselves.

Now What?

If we can swallow our pride and acknowledge the obvious—that we can't seem to get out of our own way—we can take a step forward and at least address this crisis at its cause. But what possible solution is there?

Despite our best efforts to improve ourselves or others, our basic human nature seems impossible to change.

Somehow we seem to be hardwired for self-destruction. We can come up with endless creative solutions to fix our latest crisis, but until we deal with our basic programming, nothing will actually change. We remain stuck in this hopeless place where we know that we will ultimately ignore our own well-being and do something to undermine our own survival.

I have spent my adult life teaching skills that enable people to cooperate instead of compete, and promoting a vision of a world without hatred, fear, and greed. Most people agree with this vision, but don't believe it is possible because of people's intractable nature. We like to talk about world peace and love, but in our hearts we don't think it can ever happen because we have seen that when push comes to shove, people always act out of greed and fear.

A traditional African folk tale illustrates how universal and deep seated this belief is that we cannot change our basic nature.

The Scorpion and the Frog

A scorpion and a frog meet on the bank of a stream. The scorpion asks the frog to carry him across on its back because he needs to get to the other side and he cannot swim. The frog, who would normally go to great lengths to stay away from the scorpion, considers his request, and asks in a worried voice, "How do I know you won't sting me?"

The scorpion in a sincere voice replies, "Of course, I will not sting you, because if I do, I will die too."

The frog is satisfied, and he sets out swimming across the wide river with the scorpion on his back. When they are about halfway, suddenly without warning the scorpion stings the frog. The frog feels the onset of paralysis and starts to sink, knowing they both will drown. Confused and frightened, he has just enough time to ask the scorpion "Why?"

The scorpion, sounding just as frightened and confused, replies, "It's my nature."

~~~

This belief that we will never succeed in changing our basic nature, despite it being irrational and self-destructive, is the main obstacle we face now. It is the missing link as we urgently try to address this looming crisis that might consume Earth and all that lives on it. While many of us recognize deep in our hearts that human nature is the real problem, our belief that there is nothing we can do about that makes us look elsewhere for solutions.

A parable from the Islamic mystical tradition of Sufism, featuring the iconic clown/sage Nasrudin, illustrates the insanity of this approach.

Nasrudin and the Lost Keys

A friend is walking home through the city at night when he comes upon Nasrudin down on his hands and knees on the
~~~

sidewalk under a street lamp muttering to himself and looking flustered.

The friend calls out, "Nasrudin, what are you doing on your hands and knees there on the sidewalk?"

To this, Nasrudin replies, "I dropped my keys and I have been looking everywhere and I cannot find them."

And the friend responds, "Oh, so you lost your keys. That must be frustrating. Where did you drop them?"

At this, Nasrudin stands and points over to the other side of the street and says, "I dropped them over there, in the dark."

The friend looks confused and says, "If you dropped them over there on the other side of the street, why are you looking for them over here under this street lamp?"

Nasrudin looks at his friend, bewildered that he can't figure out something so obvious, and says, "Because this is where the light is!"

~~~

The emergence of vastly improbable solutions to our global climate crisis such as colonizing Mars or genetically altering humans should be a wake-up call for us all. We are flailing around in the dark because we refuse to face the real challenge of changing our basic programming. We have determined that this is too difficult, too threatening, or impossible, and in so doing,
~~~

turned our back on the only hope we have to resolve our problem.

We are all a bit like Nasrudin looking for his lost keys under the street lamp. We recognize that the real problem is our ingrained behavior, yet we aren't trying to do anything about that because we don't think it is possible. So we focus our efforts on changing laws, promoting ideologies, or holding other people accountable because these somehow seem more possible to us.

We know Nasrudin will not find his keys under the street lamp, because he did not drop them there. He is looking there because the idea of searching in the dark for his keys is too daunting. In the same way we think changing our basic behavior patterns is impossible, so we try to change other people, create mechanical versions of ourselves, or find a new planet to live on.

Coming to our senses means realizing we cannot solve the problem of global climate change and the disruption of Earth's ecosystems by fighting our opponents, forcing people to respect nature, or escaping from our dying planet. We have to address the problem at its cause if we want to solve it.

Once we acknowledge the problem and face it directly, we can come up with new ideas to address it. Nasrudin could ask his friend to go over to the dark side and look with him, or he could try to find a light to take there. This might take a while, but it is going in a direction that is more likely to succeed because it acknowledges the reality of the situation.

If human nature is our problem and seems to be an impenetrable barrier to resolving our climate crisis, then we have to face it directly and get creative about how to approach it. We might not have a clue how to begin to change our fundamental nature, yet by asking the question and facing it directly, we are going in a direction that can actually succeed.

A New Spiritual Vision

The problem we have changing our basic nature is simply that we are not looking in the right place. We are depending on our rational mind to solve this problem, and we can't see another way. We don't yet recognize that we have another capacity, which is much greater and more powerful than our thinking mind. And we have not fully understood that it is our thinking mind that has brought us to this tragic brink.

To begin to look in the right place, we have to see our basic human nature as a process. We are not static beings. As implied by the theory of evolution, we are constantly changing, even at this moment. Every species is becoming another new more highly evolved species, including us.

According to Charles Darwin's theory of natural selection, what prompts this change is survival. And humanity has every reason to be concerned about our survival today. So, from the perspective of our current creation story of evolution, human nature must be changing. And in changing our human nature, we evolve ourselves and enable our continued survival as a species.

Here is where we need a spiritual vision to guide us, because a purely logical or scientific analysis leaves us locked forever in our basic human nature, with no way out. A spiritual approach doesn't mean new ideology or religion. We don't change by adopting new ideals. That shows us where we want to go, but doesn't help us get there.

A spiritual perspective is simply taking in the largest view possible. It doesn't require belief in magic, myth, or fantasy, but merely a willingness to admit that our current tools of science and rational thought are limited. Despite the continual discovery of new aspects of our physical world and development of previously unimaginable technological tools, there is so much more about our universe that remains a mystery to us.

A spiritual vision is not the same as religious belief. We have surely outgrown our dependency on religious ideology to explain the world to us, and we don't need a new set of superstitions to give us a false sense of certainty once again.

What we need is a language, framework, and tools with which to explore our human nature from the inside. This cannot happen strictly in the realm of science or even psychology. It requires a capacity for self-awareness and observing our own conscious mind.

Later on, I will discuss practical tools for building our capacity for self-awareness and observation of our own consciousness. But first, I want to explore this idea of our basic human nature a bit more.

What Is Our Original Human Nature?

We can begin to shift our perspective by considering that what we call human nature today might not be our original nature. One of the most well-known stories from the Old Testament of the Bible offers a clear description of our original nature and how it changed into what we consider today as our basic human nature. This story will be familiar to many people.

> And out of the ground made the LORD God to grow every tree that is pleasant to the sight, and good for food; the tree of life also in the midst of the garden, and the tree of knowledge of good and evil.
>
> And the Lord God took the man, and put him into the garden of Eden to dress it and to keep it. And the Lord God commanded the man, saying, Of every tree of the garden thou mayest freely eat: But of the tree of the knowledge of good and evil, thou shalt not eat of it: for in the day that thou eatest thereof thou shalt surely die.
>
> —Genesis 2:9, 15–17, King James Version

~~~

This story of Eden, like so many biblical stories, myths, and folk tales passed down from previous cultures, is not necessarily meant to be a literal description of our origin. Rather, stories that describe fantastic events in ancient history often include messages to guide us, if we know how to interpret them.
~~~

In this case, the message is plain as day, if we are willing to see it.

The story of Eden suggests that our original nature was unified, peaceful, and content. We were surrounded by a bountiful garden where we were connected to all things and there was no need to tell good from evil. Nothing threatened us, and we were not separate from one another or our surroundings. All our needs were met, and we were part of the larger whole of life. According to this story, this is our fundamental human nature.

Then Adam and Eve, representing all of us, ate from the fruit of the tree of the knowledge of good and evil, and everything changed. They felt guilt, shame, fear, embarrassment, and they were cast out of the garden into a world that threatened them.

The key to this story, and the incredible message it has for us, is that we lived happily at peace with all things without any way to tell good from bad or right from wrong. Our world in Eden was unified, with no duality such as we know today. All things were of the same origin and so nothing could threaten us.

Once we had the idea of good and evil, we disconnected from ourselves, one another, and the world of nature. Adam and Eve became aware of their differences and covered their bodies. They began naming everything in the garden. All things were divided into right and wrong, and we have been dividing them ever since. The result is a world where everything is separate and apart from the whole, many things threaten us, and we have to constantly discern good from evil to ensure our survival.

In this story, the garden did not change, it was the minds of Adam and Eve that changed. Where once they saw all things connected, suddenly they saw all things separate, in competition with one another for survival. This is a key to the message the story has for us.

Most of us would argue that Earth is not like Eden, because here there are real threats and we are vulnerable individuals who have to struggle for our own survival. Yet, what if we are mistaken and it is the way we *perceive* our situation that makes it either threatening or peaceful?

I know this is a big leap that puts into question our entire model of reality. Yet, the biblical story of Eden clearly suggests that it was a change of mind, not of the physical world, that transformed Adam and Eve's world so completely.

The implication is that our original nature was different from our nature today. And we can go back to Eden, or return to our original nature, by surrendering our capacity to know good from evil.

Of course, this is the last thing most of us would consider. We value our rational mind and its capacity for judgment above all else, and consider it the essence of who we are. However, what if this is not our essence or original nature, but a characteristic we acquired that fateful day in Eden?

Defining Human Nature

Our human nature, which many of us believe cannot be changed, could be defined as our capacity for rational judgments. The most basic of these is telling right from wrong, or good from evil. These two opposites form the basic reference points that enable our perceptual mind to compare and evaluate everything.

To know what something is, we compare it with something else, which it is not. This constant comparison is going on all the time and is why our mind is always busy. And to enable this process of evaluation, we use reference points that have to be polar opposites to provide us with a baseline.

Our mind is programmed to determine an absolute right and wrong and then compare everything we experience against these. In this way, our capacity to tell good from evil forms the basis of who we are. We believe this to be our basic human nature, which cannot be changed, however, the biblical story of Eden suggests otherwise.

According to this story, our original nature changed when the first humans gained the knowledge of good and evil, which gave us our capacity for perception. This implies that before this, we didn't need to decide what was good or bad, right or wrong.

Our primary nature then is to be connected to all things and part of a whole much larger than our individual selves. In our original state of mind, we had no need to divide everything into categories and figure out what everything is. The meaning of everything was apparent in our inherent connection to it. Everything was part of the same whole, and our differences were not important because we all shared a common source.

Are Values Real?

It is impossible for most of us to conceive of a world without good and evil, just as it would be to imagine a world without time or money. Yet, these are all inventions of our mind that don't exist as absolute realities outside the perceptual framework we create.

There is no *real* time. It is not actually one o'clock, or Tuesday, or January, or 2020. Measuring time is a convention we set up to organize our days, and coordinate our lives. We all agree on these measurements and so they work to organize us. In a similar way, we designate a piece of paper with the value of ten dollars, but it does not actually have that value. It works to represent that value in commerce because we all agree to give it that value.

There is nothing wrong with our values, but it is important to recognize that they are not real. They have no absolute basis by which to measure them. And the same is true for right and wrong, good and evil.

For all the effort and thought we put into determining an absolute right or wrong that we can all agree on, we have never succeeded. This is because these values, above all others, are personal and situational. We each have a different perspective, and our perspective keeps shifting. What seems right to me in this moment might seem wrong in another, and what feels right to one person might well seem wrong to another. That is what makes us unique individuals.

I know this is thin ice I am on here and you might be feeling uncomfortable, thinking that without some idea of right and wrong the world will devolve into chaos.

Just bear with me a bit longer, and give this time to digest.

Consider that this habit of dividing the world into good and evil that we acquired when our ancestors ate the fruit in Eden might be the *cause* of conflict, war, and violence in our world. Instead of making the world more orderly and peaceful, this habit of judging good and evil has made us judge one another and go to war ever since we can remember. Instead of uniting our world, it has divided it and made it unstable, violent, and insecure.

There never has been a universal moral code that resolved our human tendency toward aggression, violence, greed, hatred, oppression, or war. I am against killing and don't believe it solves any problem, ever. I would like the world to all agree that people killing people for any reason is illegal and wrong. But this will never happen. Many of you probably don't agree with my point of view, and although you would consider killing in many situations to be wrong, in other situations you would consider it right. So, who decides?

Look at any story where there seems to be a clear villain and it will have another side—the villain's side. In hindsight, many of us can agree that Adolf Hitler, leader of Nazi Germany, was a supervillain and the embodiment of evil. Yet in his view, and some sixty million Germans in 1933, he was a hero who would make Germany great again.

No matter what the situation or how gruesome the act of evil, there will never be consensus among people as to who is wrong and who is right. Most of the time our actions come from involuntary self-preservation instincts, and we all think that we are right and the other is wrong.

We each live in a world that is defined by our values of good and bad, just as it is defined by time and money. We make reference to these all through the day, and so they take on a reality to us that is unquestionable. But if we step back and look honestly, we can see there is no such thing as an absolute value to time, money, and especially right and wrong.

We are simply not able to decipher an absolute right and wrong in this world. Our struggle to do so has only caused more conflict and violence against one another. We end up living in a world where might makes right, or we invoke our image of God to justify our actions and declare them righteous. This is how we can imagine a righteous war and believe it is right and good to kill other people.

Trying to resolve conflicts by judging one side as wrong has never worked. This is because each side sees *itself* as right, so it becomes a power struggle to see who will win. Winning is not the same as being right, although we often confuse the two. And this process puts us in competition with each other, with both sides fighting to be right.

As I discussed earlier, even when a number of us agree that something is wrong, it does not stop us from doing it. If changing our habits or our nature was as easy as determining what is wrong, this would be a different world. We all do things we know are wrong, but we can't help ourselves. Simply making these value judgments does not make our world more stable, secure, or logical.

The Catholic church is perhaps the largest and most powerful institution humanity has created whose primary purpose is determining right from wrong. And we now know it has caused one of the most horrific violations of human decency in perpetrating and enabling widespread child sex abuse committed by its priests.

Surely there is no better proof that our capacity to determine good from evil is entirely dysfunctional and does not result in a safe or sane world. These reference points of right and wrong seem essential to our being and form the basis of our reality. Yet they are actually arbitrary judgments that can be manipulated by the rational mind in any way that is convenient for the ego to get what it wants.

Our Image of God

Embedded in the historic Judeo-Christian religions of the Western world is the concept of an all-powerful God who knows and controls everything in our lives. Whether we believe this or not, it is difficult to escape the notion of a superhuman figure who ultimately decides our fate.

I am compelled by the idea of God as the source of consciousness and the whole intelligent mind containing all the universe. I have found it essential on my spiritual journey to consider God as the unifying source behind all life. Without this notion, we only have a fragmented world with no cohesion or true intelligence.

However, I reject the notion of God as some superhuman being who makes judgments and decides ultimate right from wrong. If this were the case, how do we explain all the pain and suffering that befalls innocent people in this world, and all the glory and success given to people who use force and violence to get their way?

I believe it is a grave mistake to imagine God in human terms. By thinking of God as having human characteristics, making evaluations, and passing judgments, we are merely projecting our own image onto this concept. This distorts the notion of a singular source of life and renders us unable to access it.

The result is an unpredictable world without a center that could turn on us at any moment. This cultivates chronic insecurity and fear of God, and leaves us with the option to either reject God altogether or try to supplicate God for our own benefit.

It is understandable that we would make God in our image because that is all we know. We cannot imagine an intelligent being without giving it human form and characteristics. But, what if God has no form or characteristics, no personality, or even a perceptual mind that can measure, evaluate, and determine good from evil?

I like to think of God as the intelligent consciousness that contains all of us and all of life. Words and images fail to get even close to the real God because they reduce reality to comparative evaluations, which cannot represent the whole. The mind we are using to perceive God can only break the concept down into relative terms, which effectively strips God of its ultimate power and meaning.

The best way to think of God might be as the air we breathe or the atmosphere we live in here on Earth. It is the source from which our consciousness arises, and as such, it is an energy field that contains and supports us all. It is the singular unifying force in this seemingly disconnected world.

The Message of Eden

The message of the story of Eden is not about God or disobedience or any of the physical details. It is a creative and poetic way to describe what happened to us to change our original nature. We started to believe that we could tell good from evil, and we then based our entire worldview on this capacity, thinking it would make us omnipotent like God. Instead, it has done nothing but create division among us and perpetuate conflict in our world.

The notion that some things are good while others are evil *creates* conflict and insecurity, because we are constantly fighting against whatever we perceive as evil to save whatever we think is good. On a limited planet where we all share the same resources and depend on one another for our individual survival, this is insanity. It puts us in a life-or-death competition with one another that can only end in chronic insecurity and mass destruction.

What we call human nature now is essentially our capacity to make judgments about right and wrong, good and evil. We do this with our perceptual mind, the mind that is constantly evaluating and labeling everything. Most of us think of this mind as who we are.

Yet we have a story that describes a different human nature. In the story of Eden, we don't divide everything into opposites, such as good and evil, but rather see everything as part of a continuous whole. This story reveals that we *learned* to see the world in dualistic terms of right and wrong. If that is so, then we can unlearn it and go back to our original state of connection with the whole of life.

Going Back to Our Original Nature

The question is *how* to go back to our original state of mind or change what most of us see as our inherent and intractable human nature. I believe this is possible, and I am going to talk about how it might be done. But first, let's make something clear.

Restoring our mind to its original state (as in Eden) requires clear intention and dedicated effort. It will not work to merely believe in goodness or some spiritual ideal of human enlightenment. That belief can get us started and provide some measure of inspiration along the way. Then we have to want it with all our being and be willing to work for it. And that is when this process of spiritual growth gets gritty and real.

The problem many of us have today with religion, spirituality, or new-age beliefs is that they lack substance. Many of them are superficial masks we try to put over our raw animal nature to make it look like we are more loving, generous, or forgiving. In the end, all they do is hide our basic programming, even from ourselves. It is when we *think* we've changed our nature, and in reality we haven't, that we're really stuck.

Most of the programs claiming to make us better, more religious, or spiritual, aim at masking the symptoms of our human nature. We are good at pretending and making a personality to fit our ideals. And often these methods simply help us form a better mask to look good in the eyes of the world.

But pretense falls apart when things get real. Look at the epidemic of Catholic priests who sexually abused children put into their care, and how the entire institution of the church colluded to keep this horrific transgression secret. Scratch the surface of any person or institution claiming to be holy or spiritual and we will likely find hypocrisy.

I am not interested in superficial change. Some might find it attractive because it seems easier than what I am about to suggest. However, just changing our beliefs or taking on new ideals does not deal with the root of the problem. This message is for those who want something real and are willing to risk something to get it.

Tooling Up

Thinking black and white, using the reference points of good and evil, was programmed into us so long ago that we now see it as our essential nature. To undo this requires effort and focus, and this is where most of us lose interest. Many of us have tried to change and given up because it seems impossibly difficult.

Transforming our mind from one that stands apart and judges things in terms of good and bad to a mind that sees itself as inherently connected to all things is difficult. But the way becomes possible once we learn to use the appropriate tools.

Imagine going out into your yard and trying to dig a garden with your bare hands. You could manage to rip up some grass and sort out the roots and make a small plot of soil to plant seeds. However, your hands would certainly get battered, and your garden would be small and mediocre at best.

Now, imagine that I gave you a shovel, a hoe, and a rake, and showed you how to use them. You would still have to work hard and learn the best way to handle the tools, but after some practice, you could make a large and beautiful garden without beating up your hands.

Trying to change our programmed human nature without tools or guidance is like digging a garden in our yard with just our bare hands. There are tools and teachers designed to help us in this project, and using them makes our efforts more effective. Of course, we need to exercise discernment, just as we would with any new tool or teacher.

If a gardening teacher tried to get you to use a plastic spoon instead of a shovel or was trying to sell you an elaborate machine that would dig, plant, weed, and harvest your garden at the push of a button, you would be wise to look closer and evaluate its usefulness. But the fact that some poor teachers and methods are offered, simply means you have to pay attention to what really works.

Learning to use tools that enable our mind to function as an open channel of awareness, without proliferating evaluations and judgments, is a spiritual path. We learn by practicing how to release our judgments as they arise and encounter raw experience, without the constant interpretations of our thinking mind. As we practice this kind of presence, we begin to experience ourselves as we were originally, before we were all programmed to evaluate good and evil by eating the proverbial fruit.

An excellent tool for this purpose was taught by the Buddha over 2,500 years ago and is still practiced today in traditional monasteries throughout Asia, and more recently in Europe and the Americas. The tool is called meditation, and, like many tools, it has taken on different forms for different functions in different ages and cultures.

As suggested earlier there is no "right" form, and choices exist because not every form is right for every person. However, don't allow yourself to get distracted by the different forms or seduced by the idea that one form is better. It is wiser to see what they all have in common and understand the essence of the tool and what it is intending to do.

Meditation is simply the practice of redirecting our attention from thoughts to direct experience. To facilitate this, each meditation form uses an object to bring our attention to, such as the natural sensations of the body breathing. Awareness of breathing is reportedly what the Buddha originally taught and is the basis of insight meditation, mindfulness, or vipassana.

This practice works well to restore the mind to its original unprogrammed state of open awareness. Over time, it enables us to simply interrupt any thought, judgment, evaluation, or story, and let it go. As we develop our capacity for this level of surrender, we notice that the ideas and judgments we once thought were essential and true, are really insignificant.

This is the kind of dramatic insight that has to be seen to be believed. We are all in some way addicted to our thoughts and think highly of them. We are counting on our thinking mind to solve our problems, make us safe, and ensure our survival. No one can make us believe that our thoughts are arbitrary conclusions intended to create the illusion of certainty. However, when we see it for ourselves, something fundamental shifts inside us.

Teachers and Tools

The biblical story of Eden describes our original state and what happened to change us into who we are today. I find it inspiring as it highlights how we got here and suggests a way to change our fundamental nature back to the way it was in the beginning.

In addition to this, there are myriad spiritual teachings, both ancient and modern, that describe our impossible situation and how to get out of it. On my path, I have absorbed teachings by Buddha, Christ, and others, and have found in them a remarkably common premise.

I believe there are spiritual teachers who genuinely transformed their own human nature, and then showed us a way to do that. These teachers never intended to start a religion or create an institution. They were trying to help us transform our nature and go back to our original state of innocence.

In the religions that inevitably formed after these teachers left, there are still some remnants of their original message. More important, there are tools we can use today to help us do what they did. Sifting through the centuries of interpretations and finding the messages of truth is a bit like going on an archeological dig. But it is well worth the effort, even just to know that these people actually did transform themselves and that it's possible for us to do the same.

My first discovery of this nature was in a Buddhist monastery in a remote corner of Asia in 1976. I had gone to live in Sri Lanka five months earlier on an urgent quest to discover meaning and purpose. Nothing I had tried before satisfied my need to know for myself what is real. And so I was astonished and comforted upon reading the Buddha's teaching that the only way to satisfy our need for truth is through direct personal experience.

Far from teaching religious dogma or belief, the Buddha told us not to believe anything he said, but to look and see for oneself. And to enable this deep inner seeing he developed and taught the practice of meditation. This is a simple tool for insight and discovery that anyone can use to see what is *really* happening, as opposed to what we *think* is happening.

Insight meditation, one of the original forms taught by the Buddha, is simply a tool to transform our mind. It is not the only tool, just as Buddha is not the only teacher. In the end, any true teaching and practice will lead to the same place of restoring the power of our whole mind, undivided by divisions of right and wrong.

Doing the Work

The practice of meditation is simple, but often difficult and discouraging because the mind has such a trance-like hold over our attention. I remember when I was about seventeen years old, realizing that I was addicted to television. I couldn't be in a room with a television on without it taking all my attention. It made me uncomfortable that something could have such control over me, and knew I could not just watch a little, so I gave up watching TV altogether. After a year or so, my interest in television just faded away.

It was not long after this that I encountered my real addiction—my own thoughts. I realized how mesmerized I was by them and that I could not escape them, even for a moment. I had an overwhelming urge to do something about this also, but had no idea what. This led me on an epic quest in which I miraculously found my way to a Buddhist monastery, where the monks taught the skills that could free me from my thinking mind.

Knowing that my compulsive thinking was limiting me, and feeling an urgency to deal with it, brought me to the place and people who could help me. But then things became really challenging. I had to sit with my own mind and body, in stillness, for many hours a day, simply watching my breath.

I was nineteen years old and had never done anything like this before. My body ached, I was restless and bored, and my mind was frantic and wild. I wanted to leave constantly, and spent hours a day planning my escape. But something kept me there, doing the practice as I was taught, and trying to just make it through another day.

I remember clearly the first time I let go of a thought. I had never consciously done that before and didn't know what would happen. To my surprise, the thought just fell away when I turned my attention back to my breath. I didn't know it was possible to simply interrupt a thought in midsentence and let it go. I assumed that my thoughts were something I had to complete somehow. But that thought, which had seemed so compelling a moment before, simply vanished into the thin air from which it had come.

I realized then how devoted I had been to my thoughts. I identified with them and believed that the meaning of life would be revealed in my thoughts. Thinking was my holy grail and the only real chance I thought I had to understand this great mystery. The last thing I wanted to do was let go of my thoughts, and I had been clinging fast to each one of them.

Over the next weeks, as I practiced letting go of thought after thought and returning my attention to my breath, I was stunned to recognize just how arbitrary, chaotic, and trivial my thinking was. Instead of some grand master weaving an elegant tapestry of wisdom, my mind seemed to be as fickle and restless as a small child.

I was overwhelmed with disappointment and discouraged beyond measure. I didn't want to believe that my thoughts were merely random distractions that would never add up to a brilliant realization. But I couldn't ignore what I was seeing. And to back up my experience was the Buddha's teaching that my thoughts merely came and went, like all other sensations, and did not mean anything.

The World Falls Away

It is difficult to describe what happened next. I was doing the work of staying still and observing my mind. As challenging as this was, it was all I really had to do. There were no complex ideas to grasp or problems to solve. And strangely enough, this is exactly what made the practice of awareness so hard.

It was as if a process was occurring in me that I had nothing to do with. The teachings of the Buddha were completely unlike anything I had ever heard before. At the same time, as soon as I heard these ideas, I remembered that I had always known them.

With each thought I let go, a piece of my world fell away. It was hard to surrender all this, but I felt such an urgency to get to the core of reality that I was willing to give up everything I thought I knew.

I also was becoming clearer that there was nothing substantial in any of my thoughts, or the world they illustrated, and this encouraged me to keep letting go. As my world continued to dissolve, along with it went my sense of self, which I had cherished above all else.

As the Buddha's teaching suggests, this personality that we confuse with who we are doesn't exist in reality. It is a product of our thoughts. I began to see how each thought wove another thread into the story of me. In each idea or image, I was the central character. My mind was continuously telling the story of me. And as I let go of thought after thought, the story of myself began to dissolve.

This would normally be a terrifying experience, causing extreme disillusionment, disorientation, and depression. Losing our precious sense of self is the one thing most of us will never allow. I did feel afraid, and there were times when I resisted and held on for dear life. But the process was taking me deeper into a realm that felt more real and true than anything I had ever seen before.

As my familiar world and sense of self began to fall apart, with it went all the reference points that had seemed so solid and real before. Time and space began to feel strangely fluid and insubstantial. So too did my sense of right and wrong, good and bad.

I saw how these markers that had defined my world had no absolute meaning. It was my mind that assigned them all the value they had. And it became suddenly clear to me that they were as arbitrary and insubstantial as all my other thoughts.

The Value of Insight

This moment of a radical shift in perspective could be called a spiritual experience. In the Buddhist practice of insight meditation, this is insight. In Christian terms, it might be called a revelation or an epiphany. These are not merely new ideas, rather they are seeing something ordinary from an entirely new perspective.

One of my favorite examples of this is how our ancestors imagined Earth. For as far back as we can see in our history, humans assumed that Earth was flat, because this is what it looks like. It is easy to see how they thought this way, as land and sea appear to extend in all directions on a relatively flat plane. Then, just in the last millennium, our perspective of Earth shifted from a flat plane to a round globe.

It is difficult for us to imagine the magnitude of this shift in perspective, or how impossible it must have seemed to them that Earth was actually a round ball suspended in space. This is because we have *experienced* the world as round. We grew up seeing globes and maps showing a round Earth and models of Earth orbiting around the sun along with the other planets in our solar system. And now we have pictures of our round Earth taken from space.

Once perspective shifts like this, it is impossible to go back and see things as we once saw them. We can't really imagine Earth as flat anymore because we have seen that it is round. This is the power of change that occurs with such a major shift in the way we view something.

The Buddha was adamant in his teaching that only when we see something for ourselves can we fully know what is real. He understood that belief, theory, conjecture, and opinion are all merely illusions posing as truth. He saw how the thinking mind interprets direct experience and creates thoughts or images to represent reality. And none of these can satisfy our essential need to know reality for ourselves.

His teaching emphasizes the simple practice of direct awareness, often referred to as vipassana, or "seeing things as they are." The theory in the Buddha's teaching is simply suggestions about what to look for and notice as our mind becomes more still, focused, and able to see beyond the superficial flurry of thoughts.

Describing an insight or truth is simply an aid to prompt us to look for that in our own experience. These teachings are not useful as beliefs or ideals, as this keeps them in the realm of thought, and it is thought that is blocking our direct experience. This is why Buddha never intended his teaching to become a religion or a set of doctrines. Rather the emphasis was always on creating the conditions for personal insight or direct spiritual experience.

I have heard that the Buddha would not allow any of his teachings to be recorded in writing, so they would not be enshrined as dogmatic truths, effectively undermining this process of self-inquiry and discovery. And it was some three hundred years after his passing that the council of Buddhist monastics eventually began to record the teachings, out of fear that they would be lost.

The Field of Awareness

The difference between a spiritual experience and a mental breakdown might be the context in which it occurs. If the sense of self dissolved suddenly without any preparation or context, it would constitute a crisis for most of us. This is why a practice like meditation is so essential. It prepares the mind for this level of surrender.

Each time we consciously interrupt a thought, let it go, and bring our attention back to our breath, a small part of the world we inhabit dissolves. In its place is a field of awareness that is not defined by any specific object or idea. This open, spacious awareness does not arise and pass away with a subject or focus, the way ordinary thought does. Rather, it is constant and ever-present, not dependent on anything for its existence.

Most of us have no way to comprehend or experience a state of pure awareness, just as our ancestors had no way to understand Earth as a round ball floating in space. To our ordinary thinking mind, pure awareness doesn't exist because we can't see or feel it. In a similar way, with our ordinary senses, we are not capable of seeing Earth as a round sphere because it's enormous size makes everything appear flat to us.

Just as we required tools and technologies, such as telescopes, sailing ships, and spacecraft to shift our perspective and show us the reality of the round Earth, we also need tools and technologies that enable us to see the reality of our own consciousness. We tend to assume our consciousness begins and ends with thought, as that is what we see. Yet, our consciousness is much vaster and more expansive, with thought being only a small fraction of it.

This is why the Buddha's teaching emphasizes the technology of meditation, instead of specific insights. The insights or truths themselves are meaningless without the direct personal experience of a perspective shift, which opens the mind to an entirely new way of seeing. And one of the most profound and fundamental shifts is experiencing our mind as a field of awareness rather than a mechanism for thought.

It will not help for someone to tell us that we are more than the sum of our thoughts and are instead the entire field of awareness in which our thoughts occur. We will then either reject this idea as impossible, or accept it as a belief and make a religion or ideal out of it. This is how spiritual experience gets distorted by our thinking mind to become just another concept. This is the basis of traditional religions and many new-age beliefs and superstitions occurring today.

Beliefs and ideals might be exciting and can be challenging at first as they make us question our previous assumptions. But they soon become familiar and comfortable as they become our new paradigm. However, when our sense of self begins to fall away altogether, there is nothing comfortable about it. There is nothing to grasp that will relieve the disorientation and set things right again.

A spiritual path is simply the willingness to be unsettled, disoriented, and let go of everything we think we know, to discover something real beyond beliefs and ideas. To allow this radical change to occur, we need another basis or foundation of being that is *not* our thinking mind with its constant reference points of right and wrong.

A practice such as meditation builds our connection with an infinite field of awareness in which we can root our being. And being rooted in this field enables us to sustain the disillusion of self, without the pain and trauma that would normally accompany such a dramatic shift.

Out Beyond Ideas of Rightdoing and Wrongdoing

The thirteenth-century Persian poet Rumi wrote about this field of awareness in his poem, "A Great Wagon."

"Out beyond ideas of wrongdoing and rightdoing,
there is a field. I'll meet you there.

When the soul lies down in that grass,
the world is too full to talk about.
Ideas, language, even the phrase "each other"
doesn't make any sense."

~~~

In the story of Eden, this field of unified pure awareness, without divisions of good and evil, is described as our original state of mind.

As I sat in the monastery over forty years ago, and my familiar sense of self began to fade away, I was left with a profound peace and stillness in which there was no fear, stress, anxiety, or confusion about myself or the
~~~

world. Doing the practice of meditation day after day had restored access to my original state of mind. And I realized then that it was this stillness that I had been seeking all along.

In the absence of ideas of good and bad, all things were connected and appeared as an endless continuum in my expansive field of nonjudgmental awareness. It was only when I thought I needed to distinguish good from evil or right from wrong that I became narrowly focused on thoughts and ideas to the exclusion of all else.

When I am fully engaged in a world in which my task is to tell the difference between right and wrong, my consciousness becomes a mechanism for evaluation. All my attention is focused on judging everything in my experience to establish these basic polarities and distinguish good from evil. I am convinced that my survival depends on this process, and I can't take my mind off it, even for a moment.

With the knowledge of good and evil, Adam and Eve's world shrank dramatically and became defined by their capacity for rational thought and evaluation. In exercising this capacity, they fragmented their world into divisions, endlessly comparing one thing to another to assign it some relative value. And now, most of us identify with this capacity as who we are, and have forgotten the vast field of awareness that is our original conscious mind.

Lost in Relativity

For most of us, a world without the polarities of good and evil is impossible to imagine. We depend entirely on this most basic of distinctions to measure and evaluate. And these measurements and evaluations are the only way we can know ourselves and our world.

The problem is that the knowledge we accumulate from this endless process of evaluation is all relative. That is, there is no fixed point of reality or absolute truth in any of it. We can only know something relative to something else. We understand things only as they compare with other things we think we know. But there is nothing in all the world that we know for certain that does not eventually change into something else.

Look honestly at your evaluations and conclusions—everything you think you know—and you will see that most of your knowledge boils down to ideas and assumptions. Little of what you think you know comes from your direct experience. You have either adopted someone else's conclusions as your own, or come to your own conclusions about how things are. And most of this knowledge is based on arbitrary judgments.

You might think you are tall or short, thin or fat, simple or complex, fast or slow, right or wrong, but these are relative assignments of value made in comparison to something else. That you are taller than another person does not make you tall and them short in any absolute sense.

The point is not whether we are tall or short, but that these are trivial conclusions that have no absolute meaning, and our mind is obsessed with them. Most of what our mind does is make these moment-to-moment comparisons and subjective evaluations. This is how we think we are gaining knowledge and understanding, but it really only leaves us with arbitrary conclusions about ourselves and the world.

Most minds are easily manipulated and false realities are easy to fabricate because there is nothing in our world as we know it that is fixed. There is no absolute reference point so we are merely awash in relative judgments that have no real basis. This makes our situation unstable and leaves most of us with a deep anxiety and insecurity about life. To compensate, we make up something absolute to believe in, such as God, religion, science, or morality.

In the absence of any fixed reference points, we make up an ultimate right and wrong and then stick to these as if they were absolute and unchanging. This is why our world is so bitterly divided over moral issues, and we fight wars over whose God is the right one. Our mind tries to create stability and certainty by believing in a set of ideals. This is the basis for fundamentalism, and it divides our world and makes for ever-escalating conflict, which is painfully apparent today.

The Cost of Resignation

Look at where our history of living with the premise of good and evil has brought us. Humanity today faces enormous and unprecedented threats to our survival. All the centuries of Western civilization, prosperity, scientific discoveries, and technological advances have not resulted in us being happier or more secure people. Instead, it seems the more affluent, educated, and technologically advanced we become, the more pending disasters threaten us.

Take a hard look at why we face these threats, and dig down below the immediate causes, and we run into human nature. Most people believe we are like the scorpion in the story and cannot change. I can't convince people otherwise, and history will always point to the intractable nature of humans as being the ultimate cause of our demise. However, consider the consequences of believing that we are stuck in a paradigm that results in an unstable world where there is no security. The obvious result is despair, depression, and hardening our hearts.

With no greater ideal to hope for, we secretly give up and resign ourselves to competing with one another for money or popularity or whatever we think will give us a shred of security in a world where the bottom is constantly falling out. Look at the generation of Millennials and we see young people who are painfully aware of the precarious position we are in on planet Earth and have little hope for anything fundamental to change.

Here is another story that illustrates this dilemma.

A man was walking in the forest one day when he saw a rusty metal oil lamp half buried in the ground. He was excited to see what this was, so he dug up the lamp and began to clean it off to better examine it. Suddenly, a cloud of smoke came out of the lamp, and when the smoke cleared there stood a magical genie.

The genie thanked the man for helping him out of the lamp where he had been stuck for thousands of years and offered the man a wish. The man thought for a moment and said he would like the genie to build him a home on Mars and take him and his family there to live, as it looked like Earth would soon be made uninhabitable by humans.

The genie became upset and responded emphatically, saying this was totally unreasonable and impossible. He said this was way too difficult a task, the conditions on Mars would never support life, and there was no way he could do that or even get the man and his family there. He asked the man to choose something else for his wish.

The man thought for a while and then asked the genie to change human nature so people were not so self-centered and stuck in their individual stories. He wanted the genie to shift the way people think so they would consider the good of the whole and preserve Earth's environment instead of destroying it.

The genie became quiet and furrowed his brow as he pondered the man's request. He began pacing back and forth, obviously wrestling with a difficult internal dilemma. Then, after a long pause, he asked the man when he would like him to start building his home on Mars.

~~~

Many of us have pondered the same question and come to the same conclusion as the genie did in this story. And tragically, this conclusion leaves us with no deeper meaning and purpose, living hollow, hardened
~~~

lives in a dog-eat-dog world. If human nature cannot change, we are certainly doomed. And if so, then what's the point?

The Sunny Side

Despite our belief that we are incapable of change, most of us love stories that have a happy ending and show that our basic nature *can* be transformed. *A Christmas Carol*, by Charles Dickens, is one such story where the selfish and greedy Ebenezer Scrooge changes into a caring and loving person, after going through an often harrowing "dark night of the soul." Stories like this give us hope that we can learn and grow from our experiences.

A good story or movie is one that touches our heart and moves something inside us. These stories usually depict a character who faces challenges and undergoes a change of heart, becoming a new and better person. The reason these stories resonate so deeply with us is that this is what we are all here to do. Changing ourselves is the purpose of this life.

Things seem so impossible and many of us feel doomed right now because we are trying to fix the problem by working within the framework that created the problem in the first place. This strategy can't work and that only makes the problem worse.

We don't see yet that we are stuck inside a programmed mindset that defines us as separate from one another, with each of us having to fend for our own survival in a hostile world. We can't see beyond our black-and-white thinking that automatically constructs arbitrary reference points of good and bad to define who we are. And we don't yet recognize that this universal assumption about reality is the cause of the dysfunction in our world.

Perhaps someday our technology will enable us to colonize Mars or find another planet like Earth and move there. But then what? What would keep us from fighting with one another and treating our environment there with the same disregard that we have here? Isn't it obvious that we will end up doing this again wherever we go?

Restoring our original nature is not as impossible as it seems. It only feels that way because, like Nasrudin in the story, we are not looking in the right place. The framework of perception is blinding us, and we cannot see beyond it. We have the capacity to transcend our ego. It is as simple as seeing our thinking mind for what it is, and no longer giving it our undivided attention and allegiance.

The problem is that our capacity for rational thought, which creates the illusion of good and evil, is so compelling that we cannot let it go, even for a moment. And that is why it takes a crisis of monumental proportions and a truly dark night of the soul, before we finally abandon our thinking mind and begin to see the light again.

The light has always been there. This story has a happy ending, no matter which way it goes. Nothing can harm who we really are. Nothing can destroy the field of awareness, consciousness, God, or the source of life.

And the point of all this drama is to wake us up to this reality.

We don't try the impossible until we can't see any other way. The global climate crisis is making it clear now that we have no choice. We have exhausted all our alternatives and now we either change our human nature, or perish as a species, and possibly take the entire Earth and all its life forms down with us. This would surely be a tragic legacy for the human race to leave behind.

Instead, let's try looking beyond our rational mind to discover our true original nature. Let's risk our individual survival for the sake of the survival of our species, or of Earth itself, our shared home. Let's unravel the great mystery of our existence and discover why we are here and what makes us truly happy.

Let's admit that fighting for our individual survival has never made us happy and has only left us feeling more alone, isolated, and afraid. If the ship is going down anyway, let's take a radical risk and give our small selves away to save the whole.

Perhaps we are all connected to a universal source, we are not alone as we fear, and this was all just a way for us to finally see it.

Resources

Other books by Miles Sherts—published by Sky Meadow Press and available on Amazon.com.

Beyond Perception—Finding contentment in a disillusioned world

Conscious Communication—How to establish healthy relationships and resolve conflict peacefully while maintaining independence

Conscious Communication for Couples—For people in committed relationships who want intimacy and independence

Website: www.PracticalPresence.org

About the Author

Miles has dedicated over forty years of his life to the practice and teaching of insight meditation. He has been a lifelong student of human nature and believes that our purpose here is to grow beyond our primal instincts.

He teaches practical ways to transform our mental framework to one based on love and empathy, rather than fear and competition.

You can learn more about his teaching at www.PracticalPresence.org.

www.ingramcontent.com/pod-product-compliance
Lightning Source LLC
Chambersburg PA
CBHW052356060726
47592CB00020B/2798